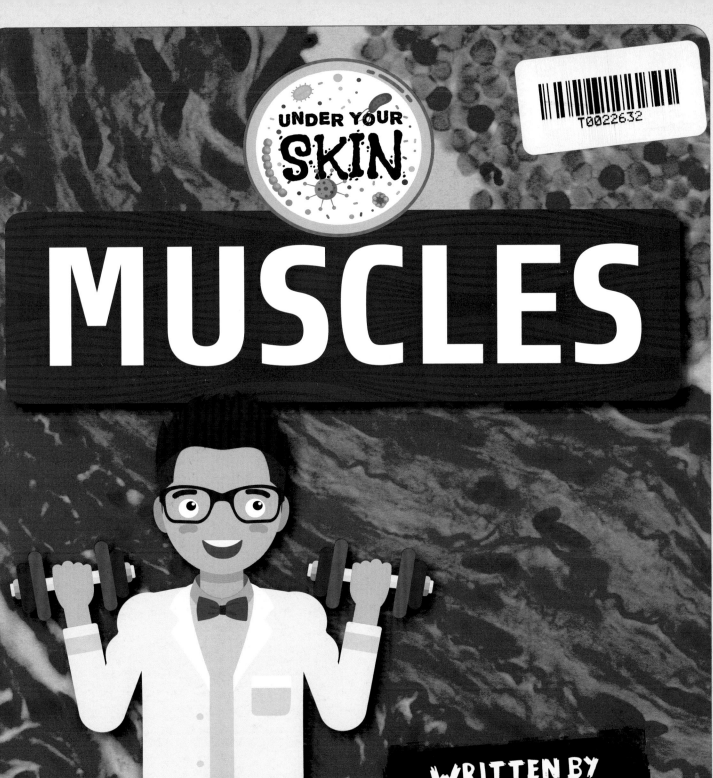

UNDER YOUR
SKIN

MUSCLES

WRITTEN BY
JOHN WOOD

KidHaven
PUBLISHING

Published in 2021 by
KidHaven Publishing, an Imprint of
Greenhaven Publishing, LLC
353 3rd Avenue
Suite 255
New York, NY 10010

Edited by: Holly Duhig
Designed by: Amy Li

Cataloging-in-Publication Data

Names: Wood, John.
Title: Muscles / John Wood.
Description: New York : KidHaven Publishing, 2021. | Series: Under your skin | Includes glossary and index.
Identifiers: ISBN 9781534535923 (pbk.) | ISBN 9781534535947 (library bound) | ISBN 9781534535930 (6 pack) | ISBN 9781534535954 (ebook)
Subjects: LCSH: Muscles--Juvenile literature. | Human physiology--Juvenile literature.
Classification: LCC QP321.W66 2021 | DDC 612.7'4--dc23

Printed in the United States of America

CPSIA compliance information: Batch #BS20K: For further information contact Greenhaven Publishing LLC, New York, New York at 1-844-317-7404.

Please visit our website, www.greenhavenpublishing.com. For a free color catalog of all our high-quality books, call toll free 1-844-317-7404 or fax 1-844-317-7405.

PHOTO CREDITS
Images are courtesy of Shutterstock.com with thanks to Getty Images, Thinkstock Photo, and iStockphoto.

Front Cover – Jose Luis Calvo, ksenia_bravo, VovanIvanovich, deepadesigns, WhiteDragon, Nadia Buravela, peiyang, hvostik, Anatomy Insider, sciencepics, Master Images – Incomible, Andrew Rybalko (Seymour), AVIcon (vector muscles), WhiteDragon (header/background texture), Jose Luis Calvo, muscolopapillare+cordetendinee(background images), Flas100 (paper scrap vectors), 4 – Jacek Chabraszewski, sakkmesterke, 5 – Jesada Sabai, rumruay, 6 – Tinydevil, Magic mine, 7 – kwanchai.c, qualitystocksuk, 8 – Victoria Shapiro, Sebastian Kaulitzki, Cookie Studio, 9 – Blueskystudio, Orla, 10 – Komsan Loonprom, EgudinKa, sciencepics, 11 – Jose Luis Calvo, UGREEN 3S, Lemberg Vector studio, 12 – Africa Studio, Kateryna Kon, 13 – GraphicsRF, MDGRAPHICS, 14 – Sebastian Kaulitzki, colacat, 15 – Emily Li, Maridov, Panomphon Damri, 16 – Veronica Louro, nicemonkey, saMBa, 17 – Alexander_P, Phovoir, 18 – julie deshaies, stockfour, 19 – decade3d - anatomy online, Flystock, 20 – Tefi, Sebastian Kaulitzki, 21 – CLIPAREA I Custom media, 22 – decade3d - anatomy online, Xray Computer, 23 – iurii, Anatomy Insider, 24 – Rvector, Artem Varnitsin, Sergey Novikov, 25 – WAYHOME studio, CLIPAREA I Custom media, BlueRingMedia, 26 – Dejms, Halfpoint, Liderina, 27 – Studio concept, Africa Studio, Tatyana Vyc, 28 – CLIPAREA I Custom media, Dragon Images, Anatomy Insider, beats1, 30 – tn-prints, Eloku, Choksawatdikom

CONTENTS

Words that look like **this** can be found in the glossary on page 31.

AMAZING
MACHINE

Imagine a machine that can solve difficult problems. It can learn complicated things. This machine can run fast and jump up high in the air. If the machine gets a **virus** or breaks down, it can often fix itself. It is made up of **billions** and billions of parts that work hard to keep it running. It keeps growing for many years too!

THIS MACHINE IS THE HUMAN BODY!

YOUR BODY IS ALWAYS AT WORK. THE HUMAN BODY IS AMAZING!

AN AMAZING BODY

You are probably not even aware of what your body is doing most of the time, but it is working hard to keep you alive! Under your skin, all the parts of your body are working together to keep you healthy and to help you deal with your daily life and activities. Do you ever think about what happens to your food after it disappears into your mouth? Or why you get a fever when you are sick? Or how you can breathe when you sleep? Your body does a lot of things **automatically.**

THE HUMAN BRAIN

Your brain, sitting in your head right now, is the most amazing part of your body. Human brains are so complicated, we still don't really understand everything about them. There are around 100 billion nerve **cells** in the brain that carry messages around the brain and body. However, the brain needs other body parts to work with it. What makes the body amazing is how it all fits together. It's time to go under your skin and find out how it all works!

THE DOCTOR IS HERE

Hi! My name is Seymour Skinless, and I am the world's smallest doctor—the only doctor small enough to go under your skin and find out exactly what is wrong! You must be my assistant. Well, you are just in time—we have a patient here who is in trouble. I think there is something wrong with her muscles. You know what muscles are, right? Well, don't worry, soon you will—we are about to go inside her body and find out all about them. Now, let's shrink you down to my size and go inside...

WHAT SEEMS TO BE THE
PROBLEM?

WHAT ARE MUSCLES?

Like many things that make up the human body, muscles are made up of human **body tissue**. Underneath the skin, muscles and tissue look like meat you would get from any animal. There are three types of muscles in the human body: skeletal muscles, smooth muscles, and heart muscles.

> Don't worry, we'll be visiting all three types of muscles along the way. Although, I'm not exactly sure where "the way" is... I'm already lost. What if we never find the way? What if we wind up somewhere gross?

THIS MODEL OF THE HUMAN BODY SHOWS WHAT IS UNDER THE SKIN.

EASY SQUEEZY

Every muscle in the human body contracts. This means they can get smaller when you squeeze them. When muscles contract, body parts move. This might mean moving a leg or arm, or it might mean inflating and deflating your lungs to help you breathe. As you can imagine, these movements are quite important in keeping us alive.

THE DIAPHRAGM (DIE-AH-FRAM) IS THE MUSCLE THAT MOVES YOUR LUNGS AND HELPS YOU BREATHE.

SKELETON LESSONS

Before we talk about muscles, we need to talk about the skeleton. The skeleton is the frame that everything else in your body hangs on to. It is made of hard bones of all different shapes and sizes. Not only does the skeleton keep you from being a wobbly pile of tissue on the floor, but it also protects you from damage. For example, the ribs around your chest protect important **organs** such as the heart and lungs. Your skull protects your brain. The skeleton and muscles work together to help you move around.

SKELETON MODEL

THE MUSCULAR SYSTEM

Often, when we talk about moving muscles in the body, we are talking about a certain group of muscles. **Scientists** call this the human muscular system. This is the name for all the muscles that are connected to your skeleton. Not only do these muscles help you move around, but they also give you your shape.

THERE ARE OVER 600 MUSCLES IN THE HUMAN BODY.

THERE ARE MANY SKELETAL MUSCLES IN YOUR HANDS, ARMS, FEET, AND LEGS.

LEFT AT THE
LEGS

Ah, here we are—the legs. These are full of those skeletal muscles we were talking about. They're in here somewhere... probably behind all this useless blood. She won't need all this blood, will she? Why are you looking at me like that?

SKELETAL MUSCLES

A lot of what goes on in the body happens without us thinking about it. But there are other muscles that we need to choose to move in order for them to work. For example, your heart beats automatically – you don't have to think about it. But if you want to scratch your nose, you need to control your muscles to do it. We can control all of our skeletal muscles.

WE CAN CONTROL OUR SKELETAL MUSCLES TO DO LOTS OF USEFUL THINGS, AND SOME SILLY ONES TOO.

MUSCLE FIBER

Skeletal muscles are made up of something called muscle fiber. Muscle fibers are long, thin, and stringlike. When lots and lots of them are put together, they make a muscle. There are two types of muscle fibers: fast twitch and slow twitch. Slow twitch fibers contract very slowly, but they don't usually get tired. Fast twitch fibers contract quickly, but they get tired very easily.

Muscles in the back are slow twitch fibers. This is because they have to work all day to keep you up, and they mustn't get tired too easily.

Muscles in the eye are fast twitch fibers. They need to move quickly, in short bursts.

HOW DO MUSCLES MOVE BONES?

To move parts of your body, such as your leg, you use skeletal muscles, bones, and tendons. Tendons are thin, stretchy lines of tissue that connect your muscles to your bones. When a muscle contracts, it pulls on the tendon. The tendon pulls the bone, and the body part begins to move. For example, when a group of muscles at the front of your thigh, called the quadriceps (kwod-ruh-seps) contract, they pull on tendons connected to the knee. This makes the knee move, and your leg becomes straight.

TENDONS NEED TO BE TOUGH AND STRONG TO PULL BONES.

IT TAKES MORE THAN ONE MUSCLE TO KICK

What if you want to move your leg the other way and bend the knee? Muscles can tighten up and get smaller, but they can't get bigger than their relaxed size. To solve this problem, many muscles come in pairs. For example, in the back of the thigh is a different set of muscles, called the hamstring muscles. The tendons run down to the lower leg. When the hamstring muscles are squeezed, they pull the lower leg back, and the knee bends.

This quadriceps is relaxing.

This hamstring is relaxing.

This quadriceps is contracting.

This hamstring is contracting.

STRAIGHT ON AT THE
STOMACH

SMOOTH MUSCLES

You can't control your smooth muscles. They work inside your body without you even knowing. They help you do all sorts of important things like breathing, eating, and going to the bathroom. Smooth muscle is found inside **hollow** organs.

WHAT IS AN ORGAN?

An organ is a part of the body that has a very important job. Usually an organ is a single part of your body. For example, your brain is an organ because it is a single meaty object in your head that has an important job: to control all the other parts of the body. However, your blood isn't an organ because it is found all over your body, and it has many jobs.

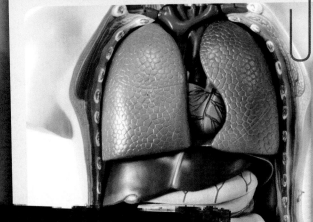

MOST ORGANS ARE FOUND IN YOUR CHEST AND TUMMY.

THE STOMACH

There is a tube that takes food from your mouth to your stomach. The food then goes through other tubes, called **intestines**, until it finally comes out of the body as poop. These tubes and organs are filled with smooth muscle. The smooth muscle contracts and relaxes in a way that forces the food through your body, like forcing toothpaste out of a tube. The stomach is lined with **mucus** to protect the walls of smooth muscle.

FOOD IS MIXED AND CHURNED IN THE STOMACH.

WHAT IS SMOOTH MUSCLE MADE OF?

The reason it is called smooth muscle is because it looks smooth under a **microscope**. Whereas skeletal muscles have lots of thin fibers that make them look striped, the fibers in smooth muscles are spindle-shaped, which means they are wide in the middle and thin at the ends. These fibers are thousands of times shorter than the fibers in skeletal muscles.

SKELETAL MUSCLE

SMOOTH MUSCLE

TYPES OF MOVEMENT

Smooth muscle can create all sorts of movement. It can push things along tubes, like in the intestine. It can churn and mix things, like in the stomach. And smooth muscle can also force things out of an organ. Some of these movements are helped by controlled skeletal muscles, but the smooth muscles are still very important.

You might be wondering why I took you to this dangerous, acid-filled stomach to show you smooth muscle. Well, it was either this or the bladder. You're welcome. Oh no! My shoe!

HANG AROUND THE
HEART

ARE HEARTS IMPORTANT?

Hearts are very, very important organs. Your heart can be found in the middle of your chest, slightly to your left. You might be able to feel your heart beating in your chest, especially when you are excited or out of breath. When the heart beats, it pumps blood around the body, through tubes called blood vessels. The blood visits all the different parts of the body. It carries things that the body needs, and takes away the things that it doesn't. The muscle that makes up the heart is called cardiac muscle.

THE HUMAN HEART

YOUR HEART IS ABOUT THE SIZE OF YOUR FIST.

UNDER THE MICROSCOPE

Just like skeletal muscles, cardiac muscle looks striped under a microscope. This is because of the shape and size of the muscle fibers. However, we cannot control cardiac muscle. The heart beats without us even thinking about it, while we are awake and while we are asleep. The heart also beats in a steady rhythm—this means it follows a repeated pattern, like the drumbeat in a song. However, sometimes the pattern will get faster or slower. This happens when we exercise, or when we feel excited or scared.

THIS IS HEART MUSCLE UNDER A MICROSCOPE.

MORE THAN A MUSCLE

The heart muscle is special because it never gets tired. This is important, because if the heart stopped beating, we wouldn't last very long. The different parts of the heart do not contract all at once. The contraction is like a wave that quickly spreads through the heart. This means the blood comes into the heart from one side, is squeezed through the heart by the wave, and is then pumped back out of blood vessels on the other side.

There are four **chambers** in the heart that blood is squeezed through.

MOST HEARTS BEAT BETWEEN 60 AND 100 TIMES A MINUTE.

WHY DOESN'T THE HEART GET TIRED?

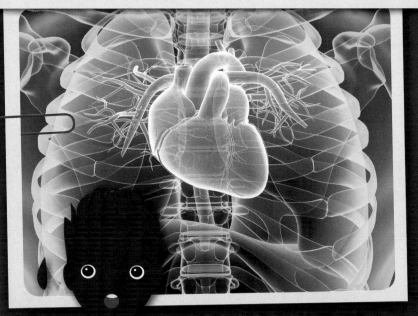

The tiny fibers that make up muscles have something inside them called mitochondria (my-toe-con-dree-ah). These are tiny parts of a cell that create **energy**. The energy is used by the muscle to contract. The heart muscle fibers have more mitochondria than any other muscle or tissue in the human body. This means there is a nonstop flow of energy for the heart, so it doesn't get tired like other muscles.

I thought the heart was going to be filled with a lot more love, and a lot less blood.

NORTH AT THE
NECK

There are many muscles in the neck. They help you move your neck side to side, backwards and forwards, and also let you nod and shake your head. The neck muscles are used all day to keep your head upright.

Ah, my assistant, there you are. We've got a job to do—help me feed these neck muscles. You know what they need, right? No? Well, you'd better read on and find out.

MUSCLES IN THE NECK AFFECT PARTS OF THE FACE TOO.

MUSCLE MENU

Every living thing needs energy to do things. Humans and animals get their energy from the food they eat and from the air they breathe. Plants get their energy from water, air, and sunlight. Muscles need energy too. To get their energy, muscles need something called adenosine triphosphate (ah-DEN-oh-seen try-FOSS-fate) – but don't worry, we are going to call it ATP for short. Muscles have many ways of making ATP, but it is usually done by breaking down **chemicals**.

ANIMALS BREAK DOWN FOOD INTO ENERGY.

MAKING ATP

There is a little bit of ATP stored in cells that can be used right away. However, it is used up after around three seconds of exercise. Luckily, muscles also have another chemical that easily breaks down into ATP. It is called creatine phosphate (cree-ah-teen foss-fate). However, that is usually used up in eight to ten seconds. Now what?

SUGAR

To make more ATP, the body needs two ingredients. One is called glycogen (gly-ko-jen), which is found in the muscle. The other is called glucose, which is a really simple form of sugar. We get sugar from all the food we eat. However, the glucose and glycogen only last for about 90 seconds.

GLUCOSE ISN'T THE SAME UNHEALTHY SUGAR YOU GET IN SOFT DRINKS AND CHOCOLATE BARS. GLUCOSE IS A TYPE OF SUGAR WE GET FROM ALL FOODS, EVEN THE HEALTHY ONES LIKE FRUITS AND VEGETABLES.

There is one more way that the body makes ATP, and it lasts a lot longer — maybe even a few hours! This last way uses glucose and **oxygen** from the air we breathe. Both of these are carried to the muscles by the blood. However, it takes time for it to get there. That is why the body needs all those other ways of making ATP first.

WE USE OUR LUNGS TO BREATHE IN OXYGEN. BLOOD CARRIES THE OXYGEN TO THE MUSCLES.

HEAD TO THE HEAD

The muscles in your face are a type of skeletal muscle. You can control these muscles, and they would look stripy under a microscope. However, unlike other skeletal muscles, many face muscles are not connected to any bones. Some of them don't even have tendons. Instead they are connected to other muscles, or even your skin. This means that even the smallest movement of these muscles can make a difference in your **facial expression**. By moving different facial muscles together, you can make all sorts of expressions.

We can make many expressions that show lots of different **emotions**.

THERE ARE AROUND 43 MUSCLES IN THE FACE.

WE READ OTHER PEOPLE'S EXPRESSIONS WITHOUT EVEN REALIZING IT.

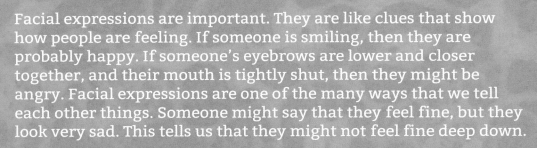

Facial expressions are important. They are like clues that show how people are feeling. If someone is smiling, then they are probably happy. If someone's eyebrows are lower and closer together, and their mouth is tightly shut, then they might be angry. Facial expressions are one of the many ways that we tell each other things. Someone might say that they feel fine, but they look very sad. This tells us that they might not feel fine deep down.

TEENY TINY

The smallest muscle in the body can be found in the head. It is called the stapedius (stah-PEE-dee-us) muscle. It is inside the ear, and it is connected to a bone called the stirrup. The stirrup is part of a set of bones that allow you to hear. When a sound enters your ear, it **vibrates** a stretchy bit of tissue called your eardrum. The vibrations travel along the eardrum and through three tiny bones called the hammer, the anvil, and the stirrup. The stirrup is connected to another part of your ear called the inner ear, which turns the vibrations into a **signal** that is sent to your brain. The stapedius muscle has an important job – when a sound comes in that is too loud, it stops the stirrup from vibrating too much. This helps protect your hearing from loud sounds.

OUTSIDE OF EAR

THE STAPEDIUS IS ABOUT ONE MILLIMETER LONG.

INNER EAR

STIRRUP

THE STRONGEST MUSCLE?

One of the muscles in your head, called the masseter, might be one of the strongest in your body. The masseter is a muscle connected to your jaw, and it helps you to chew and bite. Although it is not as powerful as bigger muscles, it is very strong for its size.

YOU CAN SEE YOUR MASSETER MUSCLE CONTRACTING IF YOU CLENCH YOUR JAW.

Hmm, there doesn't seem to be anything wrong with any of these muscles. The problem must be somewhere else in the body...

TRAVEL DOWN TO THE
TEETH

WAIT! Don't move a muscle. And let's hope our patient doesn't move a muscle either—we are in the mouth. If the patient bites down, we could be cut into tiny pieces by her giant teeth. Actually, this seems like a good time to explain another reason why muscles move...

ENDLESS CHATTER

Have you ever wondered why your body shivers, or why your teeth chatter together when you are cold? It is not an accident. The inside of your body must be kept at the right **temperature** for everything to work properly. When this isn't right, the body has tricks to help itself!

SHIVERING CAN HAPPEN ALL OVER THE BODY.

ONLY THE INSIDE OF YOUR BODY MUST BE KEPT CLOSE TO 98.6°F. OUTSIDE PARTS, LIKE FINGERS AND TOES, CAN GET MUCH COLDER AND STILL WORK.

If you are too hot, your body automatically starts sweating to get rid of the extra heat. However, if you are too cold, your body makes some of your muscles contract a little bit, over and over again. This causes some parts of your body to make tiny movements back and forth, which is also known as shivering.

HEATING UP

When muscles contract, they use energy. They turn this energy into movement. However, not all energy is turned into movement – some of it is turned into heat instead. This is why you sweat when you exercise. All that muscle movement needed for running or playing sports can create a lot of heat that your body needs to get rid of. Most of the time this is bad, because this energy is wasted. But when we are cold, this wasted heat energy can be useful. It is used to bring our bodies back to the proper temperature.

WHEN YOU ARE COLD, YOUR HAIRS MIGHT STAND ON END TOO.

You cannot control your shivering. When your brain decides that the inside of your body is getting too cold, it will tell some of your skeletal muscles to start shivering automatically. However, this will only work for a while, and it takes a lot of energy. When you are cold, you need to put more clothes on, or find somewhere warm to go.

THIS IS THE PART OF THE BRAIN THAT CHECKS THE TEMPERATURE OF THE BODY.

BACK DOWN THE
BACK

THIS IS A NERVE CELL.
THEY HAVE LONG TAILS
CALLED AXONS THAT
CARRY ELECTRICAL SIGNALS.

HOW ARE MUSCLES CONTROLLED?

Your skeletal muscles are controlled by your brain. When you want to move a part of your body, an electrical signal is sent from your brain to the right collection of muscles. The signal gets there by going through a type of cell called a nerve cell. Nerve cells are long, and they spread throughout your body. When the electrical signal gets to the muscle, it is turned into chemicals that cause the muscle to contract.

AXON

HORMONES

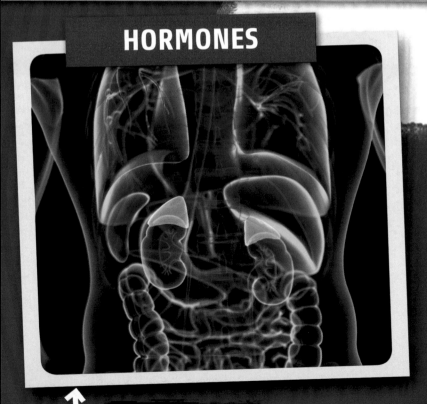

Not all of your muscles are controlled by electrical signals from the brain. Some of your muscles are controlled by **glands** in your body, which make hormones. Hormones are chemicals that are spread through blood or body tissue and tell other parts of the body what to do. For example, there is a hormone called adrenaline. One of the many effects of adrenaline is to help us breathe – the hormone travels to the smooth muscle around our lungs and airways and tells the smooth muscle to relax. This means the airways can become bigger and let in more air.

THESE ARE THE ADRENAL GLANDS, WHERE ADRENALINE IS RELEASED. ADRENALINE MAKES US STRONGER AND FASTER. THE BODY OFTEN RELEASES ADRENALINE WHEN WE ARE SCARED OR ANGRY.

OUT OF YOUR CONTROL

Have you ever accidentally touched something dangerously hot? If you did, you would automatically pull your hand away very quickly. These fast, automatic **reactions** are called reflex actions and they are different than normal movements. First, your body would **sense** something was wrong. The skin on your hand would send a signal through nerve cells to your spinal cord. Your spinal cord is a bunch of important nerves that run up your back and eventually into your brain. However, in a reflex action, the signal does not go to the brain. It is fired back to the right muscles by the spinal cord, telling them to move the hand right away! Reflex actions are important in keeping you safe.

YOUR SPINAL CORD IS IMPORTANT. IT IS PROTECTED BY MANY BONES IN THE SPINE, WHICH CAN BE FOUND IN YOUR BACK.

SOME BRAIN SIGNALS CAN TRAVEL MORE THAN TWO TMES AS FAST AS A CAR ON A HIGHWAY!

Hmm, we better check these nerves to see if they are working. Let's see, what if we—WHOA! Yep, they work fine!

LOOK TO THE
REAR

The biggest muscle in your body can be found in the rear end. It is called the gluteus maximus. It is also one of the strongest muscles in the body. You use it a lot every day, especially when running or when walking up the stairs. The gluteus maximus works with two other muscles—the gluteus medius and gluteus minimus— and together they are known as the glutes (gloots).

GLUTEUS MAXIMUS

A PERSON'S PELVIS

The gluteus maximus is joined to a part of the skeleton called the pelvis, also known as the hip. If you touch your hip at the side of your body, you might be able to feel the bone under the skin. The gluteus maximus is a skeletal muscle that controls a bone called the femur. This is your thigh bone, and it is the longest and strongest bone in your body. When the gluteus maximus contracts, it moves tendons attached to your femur, and your legs move backwards.

This is an **X-ray**

WHY IS THE GLUTEUS MAXIMUS SO BIG?

Unlike many other animals, humans walk around on two legs. This is good in lots of ways; it means that we can use our hands freely, and it also makes us taller. These kinds of things would have been especially useful to humans who lived thousands and thousands of years ago in the wild. However, walking upright means that our legs must carry a bigger share of the weight. This means the muscles have to be bigger and stronger.

THOUSANDS OF YEARS AGO, HUMANS WOULD HAVE MADE USE OF THEIR FREE HANDS TO SEARCH FOR FOOD IN TREES, OR TO CARRY TOOLS.

This is why the gluteus maximus is so big. Along with the other gluteus muscles, it is important when keeping us standing upright and balanced. The gluteus maximus is in charge of moving your legs backwards and out to the side. This means it also helps us walk and run.

Looking for this pain in the butt is becoming a real pain in the butt. Hmmm, I think we should go—all these muscles are fine. Follow me, I know a back door that will lead us out of here.

THROUGH THE
THIGHS

TEST YOUR STRENGTH

Here is an experiment for you. Find a wall and stand with your back against it. Now bend your knees and let your back slide down the wall until it looks like you are sitting in a chair. Now hold that position for as long as you can. Have you tried it? You probably found that your thighs got very tired and even started to hurt after a while. But why does this happen?

GETTING TIRED

LACTATE IS OFTEN CREATED WHEN WE RUN FOR A LONG TIME.

Your muscles break down chemicals to create energy. Most of the time, the muscles want to use oxygen to help them create energy, but sometimes there is not enough oxygen around. If the muscles don't have enough oxygen to keep creating energy, they make more of something called lactate instead. Lactate is another type of fuel for your muscles, and it creates energy that keeps your muscles working even when there is not enough oxygen. This would be useful if you were doing something important, like running away or fighting something dangerous.

THE BURN

Lactate can build up in the muscles, especially if the muscles are not getting any rest at all. Two things happen when there is a buildup. First, everything becomes more **acidic**, which makes it harder for chemicals to be broken down and energy to be made. Secondly, there is a burning **sensation**, and your muscles begin to really hurt!

THE BURNING PAIN GOES AWAY WHEN YOU REST THE MUSCLE.

THERE'S A REASON FOR EVERYTHING

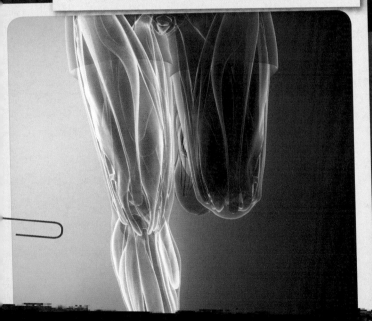

When chemicals are broken down, **protons** are released. The protons released during exercise can make things more acidic and cause a burning feeling. However, there is a good reason for the burning pain. It forces you to stop using the muscle and let it rest. Once it has rested, the muscle becomes less acidic, because chemicals are not being broken down. All of this means the muscle doesn't get overworked or damaged.

IT TAKES ABOUT AN HOUR FOR LACTATE TO DISAPPEAR FROM YOUR MUSCLES.

Pain is your body's way of yelling at you. When something is painful, it teaches you not to do it again. You'll remember not to overwork your muscles, touch a hot object... and not to bump your head on a thigh muscle!

HOP OVER TO THE HANDS

HANDY FACTS

There are 35 muscles that are used to move parts of the hand: 17 are in the hand and 18 are in the forearm. The hands are an important part of the body because we use them to do all sorts of complicated things. There are no muscles in the fingers – they are controlled by tendons that are connected to the muscles in the hand.

IF YOU WIGGLE YOUR FINGERS, YOU MAY BE ABLE TO SEE THE TENDONS MOVE ON THE BACK OF YOUR HAND.

BIG MOVEMENTS, LITTLE MOVEMENTS

There are two types of muscle movements. The big movements we make, such as swinging a leg, are called gross motor skills. The small movements we make, such as tiny finger movements, are called fine motor skills. But what does the "motor" part of this mean? The motor part has to do with nerve cells. Any nerve cell that takes signals from the brain to a muscle and causes movement is called a motor nerve cell. So, a motor skill is just a muscle movement caused by nerves from your brain. Every movement you control is a motor skill.

WE USE OUR HANDS FOR MANY SMALL, COMPLICATED MOVEMENTS, SUCH AS WRITING OR TYING SHOELACES.

GROWING UP

Babies do not have good gross or fine motor skills. But we humans learn these skills quite quickly.

- By age one, we can crawl or take a few steps.

- By age two, we can walk, bend over, and pick things up.

- By age three, we can jump and throw a ball.

- By age four, we can catch a ball.

- By age five, we can hop, skip, and stand on our tiptoes.

AS WE GET OLDER, OUR GROSS MOTOR SKILLS GET BETTER. CAN YOU DO A HANDSTAND? WHAT ABOUT A CARTWHEEL?

For the smallest doctor in the world, my motor skills are pretty big!

Our fine motor skills also get better. Can you think of examples of fine motor skills? What about drawing, playing video games, or playing the piano?

THE DARWINIAN REFLEX

BABY HOLDING A THUMB

For the first few months of a baby's life, they will automatically grab onto anything that touches their palm. This is called the Darwinian reflex. They hold on very tightly! However, they can also let go of the object without realizing it. This reflex goes away after two or three months.

ARRIVE AT THE
ARMS

BICEPS

There are around four or five muscles in your upper arm, depending on which scientist you ask. You might have heard of one of them – it is called the biceps. This is the muscle that everyone flexes when they want to look strong!

LIFTING WEIGHTS

MUSCLE GROWTH

You might have noticed that some people have bigger muscles than others. This is because muscles can get bigger with the right exercise and **diet**. This is true for certain skeletal muscles, such as those in the arm. However not all exercise will make muscles bigger. Some exercises, such as running and cycling, are all about training the body to stay active for a long time. This is very good for the body, but it won't make somebody's muscles grow much bigger. For muscle growth, it is important to do exercises that are short and difficult, such as lifting weights. If you lift weights with your arms, your arm muscles will get bigger; if you lift weights with your legs, your leg muscles will get bigger.

WHY DO MUSCLES GET BIGGER?

When you exercise, you are actually damaging the muscles a tiny bit. There are tiny, tiny rips in the muscle fibers. This isn't always a bad thing, although your body might feel sore for a few days after exercising. However, as long as you eat and drink healthy food, your muscles repair themselves. Then you will be ready to exercise again.

A HEALTHY DIET IS IMPORTANT. EAT LOTS OF VEGETABLES TO GROW UP STRONG!

After the body has repaired the cells in the muscles, it also makes those cells bigger and thicker. This makes muscles grow bigger and stronger. Exercise also helps the cells work together more. The more you exercise certain muscles, the better the cells get at contracting at the same time. This means that there is more power when you squeeze your muscles, and you will be stronger and faster.

MUSCLE GROWTH IS A SLOW CHANGE.

WITHOUT EXERCISE, MUSCLES WILL BECOME SMALLER AGAIN. HOWEVER, IT TAKES HALF AS LONG TO GAIN MUSCLE GROWTH THAN IT DOES TO LOSE IT.

Somebody stole my biceps! Or maybe I just need to do more exercise...

ALL
BETTER

Aha! Look—it's a flock of tiny birds! Who let them in? Shoo! That must be what was causing the patient so much pain. Okay then, let's get out of here.

Thank you so much for your help today. I couldn't have helped the patient without you, my trusty assistant. Hopefully you learned a few things about muscles as well.

So now you know all about the muscles. Aren't they incredible? Here are some extra muscle facts.

MUSCLES MAKE UP JUST UNDER HALF OF YOUR WEIGHT.

WE USE 200 MUSCLES TO TAKE ONE STEP!

YOUR TONGUE IS MADE UP OF EIGHT DIFFERENT MUSCLES.

GLOSSARY

ACIDIC	contains a chemical substance that causes damage to the natural environment
AUTOMATICALLY	without conscious thought or control
BILLION	one thousand million
BODY TISSUE	what organs and other body parts are made of
CELLS	the basic units that make up all living things
CHAMBERS	enclosed spaces or cavities
CHEMICALS	substances that materials are made from
DIET	the kinds of food that a person or animal usually eats
EMOTIONS	strong feelings such as joy, hatred, sorrow, or fear
ENERGY	the power required for an activity
FACIAL EXPRESSIONS	moving parts of the face to show emotion
GLANDS	organs in the body that produce chemical substances for the body to use or get rid of
HOLLOW	having a hole or empty space in the middle
INTESTINES	organs in the body that help break down and take in food
MICROSCOPE	an instrument used by scientists to see very small things
MUCUS	a slimy substance that helps to protect and lubricate certain parts of the human body
ORGANS	(self-contained) parts of a living thing that have a specific, important function
OXYGEN	a natural gas that many living things need in order to survive
PROTONS	tiny particles that are part of everything around us, but are much too small to see
REACTIONS	actions or responses to something that has happened or has been done
SCIENTISTS	people who study and know a lot about science
SENSATION	feeling
SENSE	discover or notice something around you
SIGNAL	a sign or action that shows information or instructions
TEMPERATURE	how hot a person, place, or object is
VIBRATES	moves up and down, left and right, or back and forth very fast
VIRUS	a microscopic thing that causes illness and disease in living things
X-RAY	a type of scan that creates a picture of someone's skeleton

INDEX